What is Securities Law in Kuwait?

A comparative study with United
Kingdom, Saudi and Qatar

2016

Dr. Abdullah Alshebli

Table of Contents

Introduction

In 1982, Kuwait experienced a financial crash which had a profound impact on investors and the economy. Following the crash the government embarked on a programme of regulatory involving the introduction of several pieces of legislation over the years culminating in the Capital Market Act 2010 (Securities Law).

Generally, the securities markets need special regulation because of their nature. In developed countries, the methods used to regulate the securities market differ from those used to regulate the traditional market for goods and services. This was what the Kuwaiti legislature intended when they passed a new act in 2010 to regulate the securities market.

Securities law is part of financial regulation. However, some countries, such as the UK, regulate securities as a part of the whole financial system called 'Financial Regulation', while other countries, such Kuwait, Saudi and Qatar regulate securities through separate and special laws called 'Securities Laws'.

To understand how securities law works one needs to appreciate what is meant by the term securities and that shares are only one type. Part one of this book will focus on four points. The first what are securities? The second defines securities law. The third defines Financial Regulation and the fourth is about Financial System. The second part of this book will focus on securities authorities in Kuwait, Saudi, Qatar and the UK.

Part one

1.What Are Securities?

A broad definition of a security is that it represents an ownership position in publicly traded company shares,[1] a creditor relationship with a government body or a firm (bonds,[2] sukuk[3] and debt securities),[4] or rights to ownership

---

[1] Three rights are given to an investor who buys shares. The first is the right to vote. The second is the right to take delivery of a corporation's residual cash flows. The third is the right, after all claimants are paid, to the residual assets in liquidation. Stephen J Choi and A C Pritchard, *Securities Regulation: The Essentials* (Aspen Publishers 2008) 10.

[2] Another common security is a bond issued by a corporation to raise capital. With a fixed and certain return, bonds are provided to their owners in the form of periodic interest payments in addition to a final payment when the bond matures (ibid).

[3] An alternative finance investment to bonds are sukuk instruments, which perform an equivalent function to bonds and loans in the western financial system, but which use Shari'ah compliant financial instruments. They are structured to pay a return linked to the assets that the bond has funded, so that they are not paid in a conventional sense.

as represented by an option[5].[6] Each of these categories can furthermore consist of different types.[7] For example, there are different types of shares. The table below (Table 1) shows different types of share.[8]

They are a form of asset-based and profit-sharing instrument. Iain G Macneil, *An Introduction to The Law on Financial Investment* (2nd edn, Hart Publishing Ltd 2012) 146.

[4] Debt securities are proof of a monetary debt which must be repaid according to certain terms that define the interest rate and maturity/ renewal data. <http://www.imf.org/external/np/sta/wgsd/pdf/051309.pdf> accessed 15 February 2015.

[5] The purchaser has an option rather than an obligation to buy or sell, so the consumer buys the option against a sum of money. The premium paid is the highest loss that the purchaser of an option can suffer. Iain G Macneil (n 3) 154.

[6] < http://www.investopedia.com/terms/s/security.asp> accessed 16 February 2015.

[7] Each of the securities has advantages and disadvantages. For example, one of the advantages of issuing shares is that the issuing companies do not have to repay the borrowers' money except in the event of liquidation.

[8] Rodney Hobson, *Shares Made Simple: A Beginner's Guide to the Stock Market* (2nd edn, Hamman House 2012) 3-8.

Name	Definition
Ordinary shares	Each ordinary share has an equal stake in the company and one equal vote.
Preference shares	Investors receives a set rate of interest like loans. Their dividend should be paid before ordinary shares. In the event of liquidation, preference shares should be paid off before ordinary shares.
Ordinary shares with additional rights	These different classes carry differing rights to vote or for dividends or to participate in the surplus on a winding up.
Convertible shares	Convertible to debt in some circumstances.
Golden shares	Outvote all other shares put together. Used by the government when the national interest is at risk in a privatised company.
Vendor shares[9]	In an acquisition matter, instead of paying cash, a company issues new shares to be given to the seller.

Table 1 Types of Shares

---

[9] ibid 10.

The main benefits derived from buying shares include capital gain (growth),[10] income (dividends),[11] and the ability to convert shares to cash quickly[12].[13] Owners of ordinary shares share profit (dividends), vote in company decision-making, and have the right to attend an annual meeting.[14] Usually, the buyers of ordinary shares in particular companies will be the part-owners of those companies.[15] However, there is a debate about whether the

---

[10] This means when the companies increase in value, the share price will usually go up and they will be worth more.

[11] Dividends are an income similar to interest. However, interest is paid to depositors who place their money in a bank, while dividends are paid to shareholders who buy shares of a company. Deposits in a bank pay an income which depends on interest rates. It is automatic. No one needs to approve it. While dividends from shares are not automatically paid if the company makes a profit. It is up to the board.

[12] This means owners of shares have the right to sell their shares at any time during the listing period in a stock exchange in an easy way.

[13] Thomas Anthony Guerriero, *How to Understand and Master Securities Laws & Regulations* (E- Books 2012, iPad) 78.

[14] Rodney Hobson (n 8) 3.

[15] It is generally accepted that the separation of ownership and control of the company is at the root of the corporate governance problem. How owners and managers interact with each other is the subject of

shareholder just owns the profit while the company owns itself, but this is outside the scope of the book.

On the other hand, although shares have a better return over a long period of time than other main investment types (namely bonds, cash, and property), there are three risks. There is no legal right to receive a dividend. The company can either distribute profits or reinvest them in their business or use them for an acquisition.[16] The second risk is the economic risk arising when the share price drops if people change their ideas about the company and they no longer want to invest in it, or when a company does not perform as expected. In recent years another type of risk

---

different theories, the most popular of which is the agency theory. Agency theory describes the relation between shareholders and managers as a contractual one similar to that between a principal and an agent where the latter has a fiduciary duty to the former. However, it is debatable whether shareholders are actually owners of the company. Lynn Stout stated that shareholders own a share but the company owns itself. It is a separate legal unit and according to company law, directors owe a fiduciary duty to the company. Lynn Stout, 'Corporate governance- what do shareholders really value?' (YouTube) <http://www.youtube.com/watch?v=s5Eoy988728> accessed 20 May 2014.

[16] Iain G Macneil (n 3) 134.

has arisen known as a legal risk against the company, which can be defined as a risk of legal action and the fining of a company, all of which affects the share price.[17]

There are also risks associated with the method of buying shares. There are two ways to buy shares, namely direct or indirect purchase. When a person wants to buy shares directly, they usually do it through a traditional broker, online broker, or through a financial adviser or investment manager who will in turn go through a traditional broker.[18] Indirect buying is when people pool their money with other people so the shares will be chosen by a professional fund manager. Indirect investment is known as a fund.

It is difficult to include every type of security in laws. The list of securities varies from law to law. UK securities legislation, namely the Financial Services and Markets Act 2000 (FSMA), covers these three categories with the added

---

[17] ibid 24-25.

[18] < https://www.moneyadviceservice.org.uk/en/articles/investing-in-shares> accessed 17 January 2015.

stipulation that the securities have to be 'transferable'[19] which means negotiable (able to transfer from one owner to another) on a capital market. In practice, on the London Stock Exchange in addition to ordinary shares, retail bonds and debt securities, there are many other types of securities such as derivatives, exchange traded funds, structured

---

[19] Section (102A) part 2 of the Financial Services and Markets Act 2000 (FSMA) mentions transferable securities which are defined in Article 4.1 (18) of the Markets in Financial Instruments Directive (MiFID) 2004/39/EU. MiFID directive defines Transferable securities as:

> 'Transferable securities' means those classes of securities which are negotiable on the capital market, with exception of payment, such as:
>
> (a) shares in companies and other securities equivalent to shares in companies, partnership or other entities, and depositary receipts in respect of shares;
>
> (b) bonds or other forms of securitised debt, including depositary receipts in respect of securities;
>
> (c) any other securities giving the right to acquire or sell any such transferable securities or giving rise to a cash settlement determined by reference to transferable securities, currencies, interest rates or yields, commodities or other indices or measures;

products, exchange traded commodities, covered warrants, GDRS and GILTS.[20]

In Kuwait, Qatar and Saudi, each legislature has addressed this issue differently. The descriptions are not similar, although all provide for some types of securities. The Saudi legislature, for instance, gives discretionary and flexible power to the Board (The Saudi Capital Market Authority's Board of Commissioners) to define securities.[21] The laws of Kuwait, Qatar and Saudi Arabia include different definitions of securities. In the 2010 Law the Kuwaiti legislature has defined securities as:

> Any bond of whatever legal form that proves a share in a marketable finance licensed by authority as:
>
> A. Shares issued or proposed to be issued in a company's capital.
>
> B. Any instrument that originates or proves indebtedness that has been, or shall be, issued by a company.

---

[20]<http://www.londonstockexchange.com/traders-and-brokers/security-types/security-types.htm> accessed 16 February 2015.

[21] Capital Market Law 2003, Article 2.

C. Loans, bonds and other instruments that could be convertible into shares in a company's capital.

D. All marketable general debt issued by various government entities or the public authorities and institutions.

E. The *sukuk* issued under the applicable Shari'ah-compliant contract forms.

F. Any right, option or derivative relating to any of the securities.

G. Units in any collective investment scheme.

H. Commercial paper, such as promissory notes, letters of credit, fund transfers, exclusively inter-bank traded instruments, insurance policies and the rights of beneficiaries on pension schemes shall not be considered as securities.[22]

It can be seen that the definition of securities is quite extensive. Further, by eliminating commercial paper from the definition of securities, the legislature has removed any ambiguity on the subject.

The Qatar legislature has defined securities as:

Shares and bonds of Qatar shareholding companies, bonds and notes issued by the government or any Qatari authority or public

---

[22] Capital Market Law 2010, Article 1.

institution, or any other approved securities. Derivatives, commodities and investment instruments, approved by authority, shall also be considered as securities.[23]

Qatar does not have an extensive definition of securities.

The Saudi legislature states that the term 'securities' means:

a. Convertible and tradable shares of companies

b. Tradable debt instruments issued by companies, the government, public institutions or public organisations

c. Investment units issued by investment funds

d. Any investment representing profit participation rights, any right in the distribution of assets, or either or the foregoing, and

e. Any other rights or instruments which the Board determines should be included or treated as Securities if the Board believes that this would further the safety of the market or the protection of investors. The Board can exercise its power to exempt from the definition of Securities rights or instruments that otherwise would be treated as Securities under paragraphs (a, b, c, d) of this Article if it believes that it is not necessary to treat them as Securities, based

---

[23] Qatari Law No. (8) 2012, Article 1.

15

on the requirements of the safety of the market and the protection of investors. [24]

The legislature also said that commercial bills, such as cheques, bills of exchange, order notes, documentary credits, money transfers, instruments exclusively traded among banks, and insurance policies shall not be considered securities.[25]

See the table below (Table 2) for a comparison of securities[26] and commercial paper in terms of the features of each of these types of financial instruments.[27]

---

[24] Capital Market Law 2003, Article 2.

[25] Capital Market Law 2003, Article 3.

[26] Securities are different from bank notes that are issued by central banks because bank notes have a fixed value. Muhammed Ali Sweilem, *Tools To Invest In the Stock Exchange* (Dar University Publications 2013) 12-13.

[27] Tamer Saleh, *Legal Protection for Securities Markets* (Dar New University 2011) 83-86.

Feature	Securities	Negotiable (commercial) paper
Brief Definition	Previously defined	Instruments represent the right to cash due and payable within a given time. Can be transferable by endorsement.
Important Types	Shares and bonds	Bill of exchange and cheque (certified cheque, account paid)
Value	Changing value	Fixed value
Issuer	Firms or governments	Firms or individuals
Importance	Increasing in importance	Decreasing in importance because of the of use modern methods
Essential Conditions	Usually by brokers. Trading in a certain place (such as stock exchange)	Trading between individuals. Trading anyplace
Return	Yes	No

Table 2 Comparison of Securities and Commercial Paper

There are clearly differences between securities, other investments and other commodities in which people deal. The first difference is that securities unlike goods are not produced, but they are virtually created without cost. They can be issued in unlimited amounts, because securities are nothing in themselves: they symbolise only an interest in something else. Thus, securities cannot be used to acquire goods and services: they are not a kind of currency. The second difference is that securities are affected by a variety of published information. The third point is that many securities laws contain anti-fraud provisions, since the dealing markets for securities are uniquely at risk from deceptive practices and manipulation. The fourth difference is that securities laws are concerned with regulation to ensure that people and firms engaged in that industry do not gain from their superior experience at the expense of small investors. The fifth difference is that a range of government sanctions are provided to punish those who break the rules and the securities laws.[28] It is apparent, therefore, that, because of their nature, securities need special regulation.

---

[28] David L Ratner and Thomas Lee Hazen, *Securities Regulation in a Nutshell* (10th edn, Thomson West 2009) 3.

2. What is Securities Law?

Securities markets, including stock exchanges[29], are important for the financial systems as a whole, because they represent the arteries that feed the national economy with enough money to function properly.[30] There is also an overlap between the banking sector and capital markets: both have an effect on economic development, as through them savings turn into productive investments.[31] Securities

---

[29] An 'exchange' is defined as 'a marketplace in which securities, commodities, derivatives and other financial instruments are traded'. Stock markets differ significantly from other commercial markets, as a result the effective performance of stock markets demands the implementation of a regulatory framework in the form of securities regulations. These are unlike the laws that govern other ordinary, non-securities related commercial dealings. Thomas Anthony Guerriero (n 13) 58.

[30] 'Entrance to the Capital Markets' (Qatar Financial Markets Authority)   13 <http://www.qfma.org.qa/App_Themes/AR/ABook/Introduction_to_ca pital_markets.pdf> accessed 16 March 2014.

[31] Elham Wahid Daham, *The Effectiveness of the Performance of Capital Markets and Banking Sector in Economic Growth* (National Center For Legal Publications 2013) 63.

markets and the banking system complement each other, and both should be promoted to have appropriate resources for financial investments.[32] It is important to regulate the securities market because of its potential impact on the financial system as a whole.

There is also a need for special regulation of securities because of their nature. For example, shares are intangible in nature. The holder of them owns future entitlements, rights or benefits, such as dividends, voting rights, and the return of capital, the value of which can go up or down. They are not pieces of tangible property that can be used or consumed, such as land or goods. As a result, special requirements and conditions are required by securities laws.[33] Commercial law which is the rationale for statutory regulation of commercial activities cannot provide enough protection in investment markets, because of the importance of having timely and full information in a fair

---

[32] Mohamed Helmy Abdel Tawab, *The Legality and Technical Frames For The Stock Exchange and Mechanisms of the Legality Observation* (Dar Al Fikr Al Arabi 2012) 336.

[33] Robert Baxt, Ashley Black and Pamela Hanrahan, *Securities and Financial Services Law* (6th LexisNexis 2012) 7-8.

way. There are also systemic risks in investment markets which bring various types of risks.[34]

There are important differences between the securities market and traditional market for goods and services [35] as is shown in the table below (Table 3). Because of these differences the protection of investors requires a different approach.

---

[34] Iain G MacNeil (n 3) 20.

[35] Mohammed Choukri Aladawa, *Stock Exchange in the Balance of Islamic Law* (Dar Thought University 2012) 26-28.

Type of market	Traditional Market	Securities Market
What is traded	Goods & real estate	Shares, bonds & other types
The necessity of the presence of intermediaries	Unnecessary	Important
How to implement the contract	Payment & delivery	Special way of delivery & payment.
Physical presence of goods	Usually needed	Not needed
The volume of transactions	Varies	Huge, frequent & focused
Announcement of prices	Do not announce prices for each deal	Official & daily announcements

Table 3 Differences Between Traditional and Securities Markets

Some countries, like the UK, have a single regulatory authority that is responsible for the regulation of the whole financial system,[36] including the protection of consumers of financial products and services.[37] On the other hand, other countries, like Kuwait, separate the regulation of securities from the regulation of other financial services. Therefore, the UK legislation gives the Financial Conduct Authority (FCA) more power and a broader scope. However, in Kuwait the Capital Market Authority is only responsible for regulating securities activities.

The Kuwaiti Act 2010 has 13 chapters and 165 articles. The first chapter is about the definitions of words and terms wherever they are used in the Act such as exchange, clearing agency, a security, listed company and others. The second chapter (from article 2 to article 30) is about the Capital Market Authority and its objectives, duties, powers, managing the authority board. For example, Article 3 of

---

[36] According to part 1A, section 1I of the Financial Services Act 2012, the UK financial system includes 'a) financial markets and exchanges; b) regulated activities; and c) other activities connected with financial markets and exchanges'.

[37] Financial Services Act 2012, part 1A, section 1B.

chapter 2 mentions the objectives of the Kuwaiti Authority which are:

1- Regulate securities activities in a fair, transparent and efficient manner.

2- Grow the capital markets, and diversify and develop investment instruments thereof in accordance with best international practice.

3- Enhance investors' protection.

4- Reduce systemic risks arising from securities activities.

5- Impose requirements of full disclosure in order to achieve fairness and transparency, and to prevent conflicts of interests and the use of insider information.

6- Enhance compliance with the rules and regulations related to securities activities.

7- Enhance public awareness of securities activities and of the benefits, risks and obligations arising from investments in securities and encourage their development.

The Act has seven aims. The Act mentions the aims but it does not mention the way of achieving them and nor does it explain them. The Act also gives the authority the power to pass rules according to Article 4 by saying that 'the Authority's board shall issue necessary byelaws and instruments to execute the Law. It shall also work on issuing recommendations and the necessary studies needed to develop the regulations which assist in achieving its objectives'.

Chapter three (articles 31-47) of the Act is about securities exchanges. Chapter four (articles 48-62) is about clearing agency. Chapter five (articles 63-67) is about regulated securities activities. Chapter six (articles 68-70) is about reviewing the accounts of licensed persons. Chapter seven (articles 71-75) is about acquisitions and protection of minority interests. Chapter eight (articles 76-91 articles) is about collective investment schemes. Chapter nine (articles 92-99 a) is about the prospectus for securities issued by companies. Chapter ten (articles 100-107) is about disclosure of interests. Chapter eleven (articles 108-148) is about penalties and disciplinary actions. Chapter twelve (articles149-150) is about general rules. Chapter thirteen (articles 151-165) is about transitional provisions. The act covers transactions and other dealings with securities. The Act also was the first major legislation to regulate the offer and sale of securities.

3. Financial Regulation [38]

Generally speaking, financial markets refer to the meeting place where one party has money to invest and another party has an idea of investment that needs money.[39] Moreover, Robert Shiller says that financial markets are not just about trading. Financial markets include banking, insurance, securities, future markets, and the derivatives market.[40] There are four main types of financial services namely, banking, securities, insurance and non-bank credit.[41]

---

[38] Robert Shiller, 'Financial Market 2011' (Open Yale University courses I Tunes).

[39] Mokhtar Hamida, *Privatisation Through The Financial Markets* (Hassan Modern Library 2013) 87.

[40] Robert Shiller (n 38).

[41] 'Good Practices for Financial Consumer Protection' (2012) World Bank working paper 5.

Robert Shiller divides financial market regulation into five types. The first is within a company. When a company sets its own rules, these are called inertial rules. The board, including inside and outside directors, imposes certain principles. Shiller states that members of a board owe two important duties to the firm. Firstly, they owe the duty of care; namely, the director must know what he is doing, which includes acting as a reasonable person, who obtains information, watches and is careful about his obligations as a member of the board. The second is the duty of loyalty, not simply to the shareholders, but also to the firm. There is a growing belief that loyalty has been extended to stakeholders, other people and the community as a whole.

The second type of regulation refers to trade groups or 'self-regulation', when groups of firms or people decide to pass rules among themselves to form an organisation. Self-regulation occurs when regulations are specified, administered and enforced by the organisation itself.[42] Self-

---

[42] Ian Bartte and Peter Vass, 'Self-Regulation and the Regulatory State: a Survey of Policy and Practice' (University of Bath, Research Report 17) 22.

regulatory organisations (SROs) should be subject to the oversight of a regulatory authority.[43]

Robert Shiller cites the New York Stock Exchange as an example of a trade group. As there was no organised stock exchange, in 1792 stockbrokers signed an agreement setting up the Stock Exchange to regulate the prices and the commissions. Twenty-four stockbrokers gathered under a buttonwood tree outside the building located at 68 Wall Street to sign the agreement known as the 'Buttonwood Agreement'. This agreement remained until 1974 when the government broke the monopoly. Over time, Wall Street has come to represent the financial markets of the United States as a whole.[44]

<http://www.bath.ac.uk/management/cri/pubpdf/Research_Reports/17_Bartle_Vass.pdf> accessed 11 February 2014.

[43] IOSCO Objectives and Principles of Securities Regulation (2010) principle   9
<http://www.iosco.org/library/pubdocs/pdf/IOSCOPD323.pdf>
accessed 26 February 2014.

[44] <http://www.nyx.com/en/who-we-are/history/new-york> accessed 11 February 2014.

The third type of regulation is local regulation. For example, the American Blue Sky Laws are financial regulations issued by each state. The first was issued in 1911 in Kansas, and almost every state had its own law until the 1930s. The fourth type is national regulation. To complete the previous example, after 1934, all listed companies in the United States were regulated by the Securities and Exchange Commission (SEC).

The fifth type of regulation is international. There are a number of international organisations, such as the International Monetary Fund (IMF),[45] the Bank of International Settlements (BIS)[46] and the Basel Committee

---

[45] 187 countries are members of the IMF. It has a number of objectives and functions, such as maintaining financial stability by developing international cooperation, encouraging international trade, reducing global poverty, encouraging high levels of employment, and providing loans. In addition, it monitors, advises, educates and trains the financial and economic police for its 187 member countries; Nicholas Ryder, Margaret Griffiths and Lachmi Singh, *Commercial Law: Principles And Policy* (CUP 2012) 464.

[46] It supports central banks to maintain monetary and financial stability. It has a number of objectives and functions, such as promoting discussion among central banks; ibid 465.

on Banking Supervision (BCBS).[47] One problem with national regulations is that people leave the country if they do not like the regulations. Therefore, attempts to have international regulations include: 1) the BIS in Basel in 1930, which includes 57 central banks and which suggests rules that have a real effect even though they are not enforceable by law; 2) The Basel Committee of 1974, which suggested bank regulations and was followed by Basel 1 in 1988, Basel 2 in 2004 and Basel 3 in 2010; 3) the G6, which comprises six major countries: France, Germany, Italy, Japan, the US and the UK. In 1976, Canada was added, and the group became the G7. In 2008, the group was extended to be the G20 to represent the leading financial countries in the rest of the World. In 2009, the G20 created the Financial Stability Board (FSB) located in Basel to report recommendations to the G20 about the world's financial systems. This book will not discuss Basel.

National financial market regulation can be divided into two categories, namely prudential regulation and the conduct of business regulation. Prudential regulation is

---

[47] It has a number of objectives and functions, such as improving awareness and enhancing the levels of banking supervision. Ibid.

about controlling the solvency and liquidity of participants in financial markets.[48] The conduct of business regulation focuses on the relationship between firms and customers, such as disclosure rules.[49] The conduct of business regulation includes preventing market abuse and ensuring that firms treat consumers fairly.[50] Prudential regulation can be separated into macro-prudential regulation and micro-prudential regulation.[51] The latter is about ensuring that the solvency of individual financial firms is not compromised by excessive risk-taking or other questionable practices, while the former is about protecting the stability of the financial system as a whole.[52] Micro-prudential regulation includes promulgating principles that firms must observe to ensure that they conduct their business in a prudent matter.[53] Macro-prudential regulation,

---

[48] Iain G McNeil (n3) 36.

[49] ibid 37.

[50] Emma Murphy and Stephen Senior, 'Changes to the Bank of England' (2013) 20 <http://www.bankofengland.co.uk/publications/Documents/quarterlybulletin/2013/qb130102.pdf> accessed 4 April 2014.

[51] This distinction between regulations first occurred in 2000, while in the past there was a mixture between them. Robert Shiller (n 45).

[52] Iain G McNeil (n 3) 36.

[53] Emma Murphy and Stephen Senior (n 50) 20.

which is largely an economic activity, is beyond of the scope of this thesis. For example, in the UK, the macro-prudential function is carried out by the Financial Policy Committee (FPC). The responsibility for micro-prudential regulations is divided between the FCA and the Prudential Regulation Authority (PRA). The latter is responsible for banks, large deposit-takers and others, the failure of which can impact the system as a whole. 1400 financial groups are being supervised by the PRA, while approximately 23,000 firms are supervised by the FCA.[54]

The question here is: how to regulate the financial system? For example, in the UK before and during the 2008 financial crisis there was a conflict between prudential supervision and the conduct of business supervision. It was difficult for one body to reconcile them. The former is largely an economic activity, while the latter is often performed by lawyers. A tripartite committee, which was responsible for financial stability in the UK and included the Treasury, the Bank of England and the FSA, was not able to limit that conflict. The FSA focused too much on the conduct of business at the expense of micro-prudential

---

[54] ibid.

supervision.[55] To reduce the conflict, there is a new approach that gives the Bank of England responsibility for micro-prudential supervision (shadow banking sector), which means that it oversees some individual firms in addition to macro-prudential supervision (financial stability of the economy) and its monetary policy role.[56]

There are two ways of looking at finance. The first is to focus on the theory of finance, which views financial economics as a scientific discipline. The second is about solving problems in practice.[57] However, there is no clear scientific solution to these problems.

---

[55] <http://www.publications.parliament.uk/pa/ld200809/ldselect/ldecona f/101/10108.htm> accessed 11 January 2014.

[56] ibid.

[57] Nico Van Der Wijst, *Finance: A Quantitative Introduction* (Cambridge University Press 2013) 2.

Part Two

1. A Regulatory Authority

Most countries have a regulatory authority[58] to regulate
their capital market. In the UK it is called the Financial
Conduct Authority (FCA); in Kuwait, Saudi and Qatar it is
called the Capital Market Authority. In this book, the words
'regulatory authority' mean any regulatory capital market
authority. A regulatory authority can be defined as an
administrative body created by a special law or secondary
legislation to supervise industrial, financial, or commercial
activities. It has financial independence and does not rely
on the state for funds.[59]

---

[58] In the UK, the regulations use the term 'regulatory' (Financial
Services Act 2012) instead of the term 'authority'.

[59] Zaid Aboa, *Management of Public Institutions: Foundations of the
application of administrative functions* (Dar Al Shorouk 2009) 19.

Robert Shiller likens a regulatory authority to a referee in sporting events, because both the referee and the regulatory authority can enforce rules by deciding when the rules are broken and when people should be punished. Everyone agrees about the importance of the referee in sporting events. Players sometimes argue with the referee, but they need him, because without him it would not be a good game. For example, dangerous players could hurt other players. Whilst sometimes taking risks is the key to winning the game, the referee will stop players from taking dangerous risks. Shiller emphasises that people in sports and business ask for regulations.

Establishing a regulatory authority can help to eliminate red tape ,or excessive bureaucracy, in the public sector, provide better regulation and enforcement, ease the introduction of modern methods in management and administration, provide stability, and ensure the appropriate climate is free from political exploitation.[60] The term 'red tape' has been used since the sixteenth century to describe the negative effects of bad or excessive rules, regulations and procedures, many of which are ongoing and adversely

---

[60] ibid20.

affect the performance of public organisations.[61] Such a regulatory authority needs to be effective and efficient. Effectiveness differs from efficiency. Effectiveness is about achieving the authority's goals; efficiency is about the good use of resources.[62] Resources include human, financial, and material resources, as well as information and ideas. Therefore, a good regulatory authority can achieve its objectives in an efficient way.

Securities authorities in Kuwait, Qatar and Saudi were established only recently. To assess their adequacy, it is helpful to compare them with a system like the one in the UK, which has existed for much longer, but which has undergone a number of change.

---

[61] Gene Brewer, Richard Walker, 'Red Tape: The Bane of Public Organisations?' in Richard Walker, George Boye and Gene Brewer (eds) *Public Management and Performance: Research Directions* (Cambridge University Press 2010) 110-111.

[62] Zaid Aboa (n 59) 36.

2. Regulatory Authority in the UK

The development of the regulatory authorities in the UK has passed through four important phases.

2.1 No-Statutes Era

Before the 1980s, the regulation of the financial services industry was limited largely to self-regulation, because the Investment Act 1958 was limited as a regulatory tool. It covered only a small part of the financial services market.[63] Therefore, regulation was ad hoc and attempted by largely unenforced industry codes of practice.[64]

---

[63] Financial Markets and Services Bill, 6.
<http://www.parliament.uk/documents/commons/lib/research/rp99/rp9 9-068.pdf> accessed 13 January 2014.

[64] Steve Bloor, 'After 25 Years of Regulation are consumers better protected?' (2013)
<http://www.ifaonline.co.uk/ifaonline/opinion/2258975/after-25-years-of-regulation-are-consumers-better-protected> accessed 14 January 2014.

2.2 Period between 1986 and 2001

In 1986, the original Financial Services Act was enacted, which created the Securities and Investment Board (SIB).[65] The SIB was the first self-regulatory organisation under a statutory framework, which gave it the power to oversee other organisations that regulated themselves, called self-regulating organisations (SROs). One such SRO was the Securities and Futures Authority, which regulated stock exchanges. Therefore, a mixture of the state and SROs specified, administered and enforced the regulations, with the SIB acting as an umbrella to oversee a number of SORs, such as the Securities and Futures Authority.

Accordingly, a number of organisations were responsible for the financial services industry in the UK, including the SIB and several SROs, which resulted in less efficient and effective regulation.[66] As a result of the lack of rapid

---

[65] Its structure is a company limited by guarantee, which was incorporated in 1985.

[66] Moreover, prudential regulation was given to the FSA. The banking supervision functions were transferred from the Bank of England to the

response to problems and the occurrence of costly overlaps, a number of scandals occurred, such as mis-selling pensions.[67] In 1995, Barings Bank which had been established in 1762, collapsed causing losses of approximately £827 million. The losses were caused by the trading of one bank employee who was working in the bank's office in Singapore.

It was thought that creating a single regulatory body would avoid such problems in the future. Consequently, the Financial Services Authority (FSA) replaced the SIB in 1997. The FSA combined nine separate agencies[68] to

---

FSA by the Bank of England Act 1998; Dalvinder Singh, *Banking Regulation of the UK and the US Financial Markets* (Ashgate 2007) 15.

[67] Steve Bloor (n 64).

[68] 1- Building Societies Commission; 2- Friendly Societies Commission; 3- Insurance Directorate; 4- Registry of Friendly Societies; 5- Bank of England's Supervision and Surveillance Division; 6- Investment Management Regulatory Organisation; 7- Personal Investment Authority; 8- Securities and Future Authority; 9- Securities and Investment Board.

regulate the whole financial services industry in the UK.[69] The FSA was a company limited by guarantee.[70] The Financial Services and Market Act 2000 (FSMA) gave the FSA its objectives and its powers. The new statutory system provided more protection to investors. The FSA was given more enforcement power and was authorised to impose strong fines.[71]

2.3 Period between 2001 and 2012

On 30 December 2001, Chancellor of the Exchequer Gordon Brown agreed to the independence of the FSA from the government, although it had to be properly accountable to the government, Parliament and to other stakeholders. He emphasised the advantage of having such an independent body for business and for consumers,

---

[69]<http://www.publications.parliament.uk/pa/ld200809/ldselect/ldecona f/101/10108.htm> accessed 11 January 2014.

[70] Company NO 1920623.

[71] Financial Markets and Services Bill (n63) 21.

according to a letter sent to Sir Howard Davies, the Chairman of the FSA.[72]

To sum up, in 2001, self-regulatory organisations (SROs) were replaced by a single statutory regulatory authority called the FSA. The FSA's responsibility was for regulating banks and providers of financial services. Theoretically, it had two roles. One was the prudential regulation of all of the above institutions; the other was the regulation of how they conducted their business. The FSA was an independent body and was accountable to Parliament. However, the FSA was not part of the Bank of England which was solely responsible for making financial policy, and the Treasury was responsible for passing the necessary statutory instruments to empower the FSA. The financial crisis of 2007-2008 highlighted some failings in these arrangements. The FSA had focused on the conduct of business at the expense of prudential regulation. This prompted the government to introduce a different structure for the regulation of financial activities in 2012.

---

[72] <http://webarchive.nationalarchives.gov.uk/+/http://www.hm-treasury.gov.uk/newsroom_and_speeches/press/2001/press_144_01.cfm> accessed 11 January 2014.

2.4 Period After 2012

Under the new structure, the responsibility of the Bank of England[73] would no longer be limited to financial policy, but would also include the micro-prudential regulation of insurers, deposit takers and major investment firms through the creation of a Prudential Regulation Authority (PRA)[74] to promote their safety and soundness and minimise adverse effects on the stability of the financial system. In addition, the macro-prudential regulation of the financial systems as a whole would be undertaken by the newly created Financial Policy Committee (FPC). The PRA is now a subsidiary of the Bank of England, unlike the FSA.

---

[73] In addition, the Banking Act 2009 gave the Bank of England the responsibility for financial stability, which would not work effectively without allocating to it the responsibility for micro-prudential supervision. Its augmented responsibilities and corresponding authority clearly put the Bank of England in charge.

[74] Emma Murphy and Stephen Senior, 'The Changes to the Bank of England', <http://www.bankofengland.co.uk/publications/Documents/quarterlybulletin/2013/qb130102.pdf> accessed 16 January 2014.

The Financial Services Act 2012 created two regulators, the FCA and the PRA.[75] Although the FCA is not part of the Bank of England, the PRA is, and it is responsible for the supervision and the prudential regulation of banks, major investment firms, building societies, credit unions and insurers, promoting safety and soundness to those firms and protecting policyholders.[76] The chair of the PRA is the Governor of the Bank of England, and the chief executive is the Deputy Governor for Prudential Regulation.[77]

The Financial Conduct Authority (FCA) has been created as a separate institution from the Bank of England to regulate the conduct of financial services firms. The FCA's duties include preventing market abuse and ensuring that financial firms treat their customers fairly. Its three major objectives are 1) protecting consumers; 2) promoting the integrity of the financial system; and 3) promoting effective competition. It is also responsible for the micro-prudential regulation of those financial services that are not supervised

---

[75] Financial Services Act 2012 sch 3A part 2.

[76] <http://www.bankofengland.co.uk/pra/pages/default.aspx> accessed 11 January 2014.

[77] Financial Services Act 2012 Schedule 1ZB s2.

by the PRA, such as, for example, asset managers, hedge funds, many brokers, dealers, independent financial advisers, and listed companies.

3. Regulatory Authority in Kuwait, Qatar and Saudi

Kuwait, Qatar and Saudi describe their regulatory authorities as independent bodies. In Kuwait, the law states that the authority is an independent body having a legal personality and that it is overseen by a Minister of Trade and Industry.[78] In Saudi Arabia, the law mentions that the authority has financial and administrative autonomy and must report to the President of the Council of Ministers and that it has a legal personality.[79] In Qatar, according to Article 4 of Qatari Law 2012, the Authority has financial and administrative independence and a legal personality.

---

[78] Capital Market Law 2010, Article 2.

[79] Capital Market Law 2003, Article 4.

The Authority must report to the Governor of Qatar's Central Bank.[80]

Although the term 'independence' is used, careful analysis of the text hereunder will show the extent to which this is true. To that end, the soundness and independence of the regulatory authorities in Kuwait, Qatar and Saudi will be assessed in terms of their composition, funding arrangements, accountability and freedom of action from political and commercial interference.

3.1 Composition

The following section discusses the members of the board of the Authority.

The regulatory authority is administered by a board called the Board of Commissioners. In Kuwait, the board consists of five full-time members. An Emiri Decree is issued to appoint them, and it specifies the chairman and the deputy

---

[80] Qatar Financial Market Authority Law No 8 of 2012, Article 3.

chairman.[81] Article 12 mentions that the Emiri Decree determines the board's salaries and benefits. In Saudi, the board of the Capital Market Authority (five members) is appointed by Royal Order. It determines their salaries and financial benefits and specifies the chairman and the deputy chairman.[82]

The Qatari legislation is unlike Saudi and Kuwaiti legislation regarding the appointment of the board. Although Qatari Law 2012 mentions in Article 6 that the appointment of the board has to be determined by Emir Decree, the majority of the board's seven members are known in advance, so that the Emiri Decree has no real impact. Article 6 states that the chairman of the board and the deputy chairman are the Governor and the Deputy Governor of the Qatar Central Bank. The Governor selects two experienced people. Two further members represent the Ministry of Economy and Finance and the Ministry of Business and Trade, respectively. The last of the seven members is the chief executive officer of the Qatar Financial Centre Regulatory Authority (QFCRA).

---

[81] Capital Market Law 2010, Article 6.

[82] Capital Market Law 2003, Article 7.

Clearly, the Qatar legislation has realised the effects of shadow bank institutions (non-bank financial intermediaries that provide services similar to traditional banks) on the financial systems as a whole, thus giving the central bank more power by appointing the governor and the deputy governor of the central bank as the chairman and deputy chairman of the board of the authority, which could affect the conduct of business.

Qatari legislation is also unlike Saudi and Kuwaiti legislation in that the members of the authority board are not full-time. They perform their duties in addition to their main employment functions,[83] while in Kuwait and Saudi they are full-time. Qatari legislation is also unlike Saudi[84] and Kuwaiti[85] legislation regarding the post of the chairman and the chief executive. In the Qatari authority, they are separate posts, while in Kuwait and Saudi, they are the

---

[83] Qatar Financial Market Authority Law No. 8 of 2012, Article 6.

[84] In Saudi, according to Article 11 of the 2003 Law, the same person holds the positions of chairman of the board and chief executive.

[85] In Kuwait, according to Article 8 of Law No. 7 of 2010, the same person holds the positions of chairman of the board and chief executive.

same. According to Article 17 of the Qatari Law 2012, since the chief executive shall not be a member of the board appointed by Emiri Decree upon a proposal from the governor, the chairman of the board suggests the name of the chief executive.

Despite the fact that Qatari legislation has successfully separated the chairman from the chief executive, two important points have been ignored. First, the members of the board are not full-time, which may cause a conflict of interest and a lack of complete knowledge of the nature of their functions. Second, the chief executive is not a member of the board, which may cause poor communication with the board.

In the UK, by comparison, the board that governs the FCA is appointed by several parties.[86] A chair (non-executive member), a chief executive[87] and at least one other member

---

[86] Financial Services Act 2012, Schedule 1ZA s2.

[87] The chief executive of the FCA is also a member of the PRA governing body under the Financial Services Act 2012 Schedule 1ZB s3.

are appointed by the Treasury. The Bank of England Deputy Governor for prudential regulation is a non-executive member of the board. Two members are appointed jointly by the Secretary of State and the Secretary of the Treasury (non-executive members). The majority of the board members must be non-executive members.

The appointment of the board members is subject to the Code of Practice for Ministerial Appointment to Public Bodies 2012.[88] Kuwait, Qatar and Suadi have no such code, and there is no limit to the numbers on the board. Currently, the FCA board is made up of four executive members and eight non-executive members.[89] The roles of

---

[88] Sir David Normington, the Commissioner for Public Appointments, who is independent of the civil service and the government and is appointed by the Queen, says: 'My role as a regulator is to ensure the best people get appointed to public bodies free of personal and political patronage'. The code of practice for ministerial appointment to public bodies 2012 focuses on three basic principles: merit, fairness and openness.
<http://publicappointmentscommissioner.independent.gov.uk/> accessed 22 February 2014.

[89] <http://www.fca.org.uk/about/structure> accessed 11 January 2014.

the chair and the chief executive are not exercised by the same person.[90] The 2012 Act does not explicitly provide for the separation of the two posts, but section 3 of Schedule 1ZA mentions that the chair is to be a non-executive member. In the UK, the Treasury determines the terms of service of the board members[91] and has the power to remove the appointed members in some circumstances.[92] The remuneration in the UK for non-executive board members is determined by the Treasury, while the remuneration for the executive board is determined by the FCA.[93]

With regard to the age of retirement of the board members, Kuwait's Article 10 of the 2010 Law states the reasons for a board member vacating a position as death, disability or resignation. It also mentions a number of circumstances

---

[90] FCA Report 'Corporate Governance of the Financial Conduct Authority Adopted by resolution of the Board' (2013) 5. <http://www.fca.org.uk/static/documents/fca-corporate-governance.pdf> accessed 9 January 2014.

[91] Financial Services Act 2012, Schedule 1ZB s3.

[92] ibid Schedule 1ZA s4.

[93] Financial Services Act 2012, Schedule 1ZA s7.

that will require a person to vacate his or her position, one of which is the issuance of a final judgment about the person's bankruptcy. Therefore, the article does not include the age of retirement, which is a subject of dispute. While Kuwaiti law extends the age of retirement of judges, prosecutors, and the Fatwa and Legislature,[94] the situation is not same for the board members. As a result, there is no extensive regulation of retirement age, and the age of retirement is not included as a reason for vacating a position. It could be said that there is no retirement age for the board members in Kuwait, and the age is subject to the Emir, since he appoints them. The retirement age in Kuwait is 60. Experienced people over 60 still have a lot to offer and can fulfil a useful role.

3.2 Funding Arrangements

The following discussion concerns the regulatory authorities' budget, financial resources and maintaining reserves.

---

[94] According to the Emiri Decree No 124 of 1992 concerning degrees and salaries of judges, prosecutors, and the Fatwa and Legislature.

In Kuwait, the Authority has an independent budget[95] that does not need to be adopted by the relevant minister. However, in Saudi, according to Article 14 of Law 2003, the Authority has a separate annual budget that is submitted by the Minister of Finance. In Qatar, the Authority's budget is part of the state's general budget.[96] Therefore, the budgets of the Saudi and Qatari authorities are part of the government budget system, while in Kuwait, the authority has an independent budget, because it is not part of the government's general budget and does not need any approval. However, some argue that this is not the case with other authorities, such as the Youth and Sport Public Authority[97] and the Public Authority for Investment.[98] The full independence of the regulatory authority budget is resented by some people, who feel that it should be subject to some of the same restrictions as other authorities. An example is discussed in an article published on 10 November 2013 entitled 'Budget war is renewed between the Authority and the Ministry of Finance'. The Kuwaiti

---

[95] Capital Market Law 2010, Article 18.

[96] Qatar Financial Market Authority Law No. 8 of 2012, Article 2.

[97] Emiri Decree No 43 1992, Article 10.

[98] Emiri Decree No 47 1982, Article 10.

Ministry of Finance insists that the Authority's budget should be approved by the Minister of Finance, while the Authority asserts that its budget is not subject to the approval of the Ministry of Finance.[99]

In Kuwait, the financial resources of the Authority mentioned in Article 19 of the 2010 Law include (1) fees and (2) all other resources that are raised from exercising its activities or recruiting its reserves. Consequently, in Kuwait, there is no funding by the government. However, the Saudi authority is partly funded by the government and partly by industry. Article 13 of Law 2003 determines the financial resources of the Authority, including (1) fees for services and commissions charged by the authority; (2) fees for using its facilities; (3) a return on its funds and proceeds from the sale of its assets; (4) fines and financial penalties for breaching the 2003 Law; (5) funds provided by the government; and (6) all other resources determined by the board. The Qatari Authority is also partly funded by the government and partly by the industry. Article 23 of Law 2012 determines the financial resources of the authority,

---

[99] <http://www.alraimedia.com/Articles.aspx?id=464717> accessed 10 February 2014.

including (1) financial assistance by the government; (2) fees for services charged by the Authority; (3) fines and financial penalties for breaching the 2012 Law; and (4) all other resources that are raised by the Authority from the exercise of its activities or from recruiting its reserves.

In Saudi, the Authority should maintain a general reserve that is equal to double the amount of the previous annual budget. Surplus funds should be remitted to the Finance Ministry.[100] In Kuwait, Article 21 of the 2010 Law gives the Authority the power to maintain sufficient monetary reserves to ensure its financial stability over the long term without any limitation and transfer the surplus to the state public treasury. In Qatar, Article 23 of the Law 2012 gives the Authority the power to maintain sufficient monetary reserves to ensure its financial stability over the long term without any limitation. Unlike Kuwaiti and Saudi law, the Qatari legislation does not mention transferring the surplus to the state public treasury.

---

[100] Capital Market Law 2003, Article 14.

The Kuwaiti and Qatari authorities are allowed to use their reserves, while this is not allowed in Saudi.[101] In Kuwait, this is inconsistent with the text of Article 24, which states that the Authority shall not engage in any commercial activities, lend money, or issue or invest in securities. Therefore, how can it use its funds?

In comparison, in the UK, the financial services companies, which are regulated, completely fund the FCA. It also has the power to keep sufficient reserves.[102] It does not receive any government funding. However, civil penalties go to the Treasury after deducting the enforcement costs.[103] In Saudi and Qatar, the funding from civil penalties is part of the financial resources, which could cause a conflict of interests because the authority might be tempted to increase

---

[101] According to Article 4 of the Capital Market Law 2003, the Authority does not allow any of the following four actions: (1) engaging in any commercial activities; (2) acquiring, owning or issuing securities; (3) lending or borrowing funds; and (4) being part of any project to earn profits.

[102] FCA Article 'Power to raise fees'
<http://www.fca.org.uk/about/how-we-are-funded/fees> accessed 2 January 2014.

[103] Financial Services Act 2012, Schedule 1ZA s20.

the number of financial penalties prompted not by a civil wrong but by the need to boost its revenue for budgetary reasons.

3.3 Accountability

In this context, independence does not mean freedom from accountability. The following section addresses to whom a regulatory authority reports.

In the UK, the FCA is an independent body, but it is accountable to the Treasury. For example, the FCA must prepare a report for the Treasury at least once a year, and the Treasury must then submit this report to Parliament.[104]

In Qatar, the regulatory Authority must report to the Governor of the Central Bank.[105] In Saudi, the Authority has to report to the President of the Council of Ministers[106];

---

[104] Financial Services Act 2012, Schedule 1ZA s11.

[105] 2012 Law, Article 3.

[106] 2003 Law, Article 4.

in Kuwait, the Authority is overseen by the Minister of Trade and Industry[107] and must report once a year to the relevant minister and submit the report to the cabinet.[108]

While some may consider reporting to someone to be different to being overseen by that person, this is not the case in Kuwait. For example, the Youth and Sport Public Authority is overseen by a minister,[109] while the Public Authority for Investment also reports to a minister.[110]

In Kuwait, according to Article 22 of the 2010 Law, the Authority is committed to keeping its accounts and records. This is also the situation in Qatar.[111] In the UK, the FCA is responsible for recording and safe-keeping all decisions made in the exercise of its functions,[112] and a record of

---

[107] 2010 Law, Article 2.

[108] ibid Article 25.

[109] Emiri Decree No 43 of 1992, Article 1.

[110] Emiri Decree No 47 of 1982, Article 1.

[111] 2012 Law, Article 26.

[112] Financial Services Act 2012, Schedule 1ZA s9.

each governing body meeting must be published.[113] It would be better if Kuwaiti law required publication of the Authority's meeting reports to achieve transparency. There is a saying that 'sunshine is the best disinfectant'.

Qatari Law 2012 Article 27 says that the Authority is subject to control by the Audit Bureau; in Kuwait, the Authority is subject to control by the Audit Bureau[114] after the event and not prior to the event.[115] The Saudi law does not mention any prior or subsequent control. In the UK, the FCA must send its annual accounts to the Comptroller and the Auditor General to be examined, certified and a report made about these accounts, after which the Comptroller and the Auditor General must send a copy of the report to the Treasury, after which the Treasury submits a copy of the certified accounts and the report to Parliament.

---

[113] ibid s10.

[114] The Kuwaiti Audit Bureau reports to Kuwait's Parliament, aiming to maintain effective control over public funds. Article 3 of Law No 30 of 1964 concerning establishing the Audit Bureau states that financial control includes, *inter alia*, public bodies of state with a legal personality.

[115] Capital Market Law 2010, Article 23.

In conclusion, Kuwaiti law gives the Kuwaiti Capital Market Authority financial and administrative independence, especially with respect to board appointments and its budget and financial resources. In contrast, Saudi law gives administrative independence in terms of appointing the board, while the financial resources and its budget remain under government control. Qatari law does not give the Authority complete independence in terms of appointing the board, its budget and its financial resources.

4. Sound Legal Framework

The regulatory framework needs to have a legal basis (laws, rules, codes) and effective monitoring or policing of compliance and enforcement of any breach of the laws, rules or codes. These two roles are usually in the hands of a specialised body or a regulatory authority. In the UK, these roles are performed by the FCA and the PRA. In Kuwait, Saudi and Qatar, such a body are usually referred to as a Capital Market Authority.

Generally speaking, when a financial system works well, it will help people. However, sometimes bad behaviour, deliberate or unintentional, occurs that includes action in the market, such as market abuse; action by a business itself, such as bad behaviour by one or more managers; and action by others, such as majority shareholders, who have more power than the small consumers.

A regulatory authority that oversees the capital market has a further role to play in that it can suggest continuous improvements in securities legislation as companies and others find more ways to circumvent the law at the expense of the investors. In addition to suggesting improvements to the law, a regulatory authority can make 'rules' that have the force of law.[116] This is also known as secondary

---

[116] The law gives the regulatory authority in the GCC countries the power to make rules similar to the UK. In Kuwait, Article 4 Part 1 states that the authority board shall issue rules and regulations that are necessary to implement this law. In Saudi, Article 6 Parts 2, 12, and 13 of Saudi Law 2003 mentions that the authority shall issue regulations, decisions, and instructions and shall set procedure. In Qatar, the board shall issue various regulations to achieve its objectives according to Article 8 Part 4 of Law 2012. In the UK, one of the FCA's functions is rule-making according to the Financial Services Act 2012 Part 1A

legislation.[117] In the UK, there are two categories of legislation. Primary legislation consists of 'statutes' that are enacted by Parliament. The second category consists of secondary legislation, known as 'delegated or subordinate legislation', which occurs when the law-making power is delegated by Parliament to a minister or local authority or semi-public organisation.[118] The legislation that gives the rule-making power is called the Parent Act.[119]

Therefore, there is primary and secondary legislation, and a regulatory authority can recommend changes to primary legislation and implement secondary legislation.

---

inside Part 2 Section 1B, 6, and the same Act also gives the Prudential Regulation Authority (PRA) the power to make rules.

[117] Paul Nelson, *Capital Markets Law and Compliance: the Implications of MiFID* (Cambridge University Press 2011) 4.

[118] Emily Finch, Stefan Fafinski, *English Legal System* (4th edn, Pearson 2013) 10.

[119] <http://www.soas.ac.uk/library/subjects/law/research/file70251.pdf > accessed 28 February 2015.

4.1 How Can A Regulatory Authority Help to Improve the Law?

This section will consider how a regulatory authority can improve the quality of the law to combat this crime effectively.

Several improvements can help the enforcement system, such as expert judges and criminal authorities who are expert in financial matters[120] and case settlement. These are the key to effective enforcement that increases the level of confidence and credibility.[121] These three issues: expert legal professionals, the court system,[122] and private enforcement are beyond the scope of the book.

---

[120] Ana Carvajal, Jennifer Elliott, The Challenge of Enforcement in Securities Markets: Mission Impossible? (International Monetary Fund (IMF) working paper 2009 18.

[121] ibid 21.

[122] For example, Kuwaiti Law No. 7 of 2010 mentions Article 108 to Article 116 for establishing a specialised court for securities activities called the Capital Market Court. The details of these Articles are beyond the scope of this book.

One feature of financial crimes is the difficulty involved in enumerating them, because they vary from state to state and from time to time.[123] Many activities can be classed as financial market crime, one of which is market abuse. Furthermore, market abuse covers a wide range of illegal deeds.[124] Therefore, an authority should suggest improvements to the law that are as wide-ranging.

This is the situation in Kuwait, Saudi and Qatar. In Kuwait, Article 4 Part 1 mentions that the board shall issue recommendations and studies to develop laws that help to achieve authority objectives. In Qatar, according to Article 8 Part 8 of Law 2012, the board shall suggest laws that assist the authority's goals. In Saudi, although Saudi Law 2003 does not mention any power to suggest laws, Part 4 of Article 6 allows the authority to give advice and recommendations.

---

[123] Montasser Hamouda, *Economic Crimes* (Dar Elgamaa Elgadida 2010) 53.

[124] Stuart Bazley, *Market Abuse Enforcement and Procedure* (Bloomsbury Professional 2013) 3.

The situation is different between Kuwait, Saudi, Qatar and the UK. In the UK, the regulation is not limited to securities. Banks, insurance companies and financial advisers are all regulated. In contrast, in Kuwait, Saudi, Qatar regulation is limited to the securities market alone.

One function of a regulatory authority is intelligence, which is a two-part task. One part is alerting the authority about potential concerns; the second is gathering evidence.[125] The first part, which is supervisory in nature, means discovering breaches of regulations. Supervision programmes aim to identify, deter and prevent problems. Sometimes, it is hard to distinguish among these tasks. The term 'enforcement to compliance' is used for the two parts of the authority's task.

A clear mandate to enforce the laws and regulations should be granted to the authority by the securities law.[126] In the UK, the FCA has a wide range of enforcement powers, including the imposition of criminal, civil or administrative

---

[125] ibid 67.

[126] Ana Carvajal, Jennifer Elliott (n 120) 13.

sanctions against companies or individuals who do not meet the required standards.[127]

It is not helpful to list all possible abuses in financial markets. In the UK, dealing with financial crime is a very important objective of the FCA authority. One way is to involve the firms in fighting this crime by monitoring, detecting and preventing financial crime, such as fraud, money laundering, bribery and corruption, and disclosing false or secret information.[128] In addition, an enforcement programme aims to detect and punish non-compliance and to deter such action in the future. This includes investigating, obtaining evidence and interviewing witnesses, gathering information from third parties such as telephone companies and Internet providers, and accessing bank accounts. All of these actions require that the regulatory authority have the legal power to carry them out.

---

[127] < http://www.fca.org.uk/firms/being-regulated/enforcement/how-we-enforce-the-law> accessed 15 February 2014.

[128] FCA Article 'Fighting Financial Crime'
<http://www.fca.org.uk/about/what/protecting/financial-crime > accessed 2 January 2014.

In the UK, the power of investigation includes such varied action as sanctions for failure to comply under section 177 of the FSMA 2000, gathering information under section 165, obtaining search warrants under section 176, and interviewing witnesses. For example, in an insider dealing investigation, two kinds of persons can be interviewed. The first is a potential witness. The interview with such a person can be compulsory or voluntary. The second kind of person is the subject of the investigation.[129] In addition, although disclosing the details of customer accounts is not generally allowed in the UK, section 175 FSMA 2000 allows it in certain circumstances. A study of these circumstances is beyond the scope of this book.

Unlike the UK, the situation in Kuwait, Saudi, Qatar countries need to be improved. The situations in Saudi, Qatar and Kuwait are all different. In Saudi, Article 5 Part c of Saudi Law 2003 gives the Authority the power to investigate, take evidence, and subpoena witnesses. Part 12 of Article 6 gives the Authority the power to conduct inquiries and investigations. However, these powers are for

---

[129] Sarah Clarke, *Insider Dealing: Law and Practice* (Oxford University Press 2013) 244- 247.

enforcement of the 2003 law's provisions, regulations and rules. Therefore, the scope of the power is limited to applying Law 2003. It would be better if these powers were applicable for every breach of the financial markets. In Qatar, the Authority has the right to investigate, inspect[130] and prove by all means, including electronic devices.[131] In Kuwait, Article 3 Part 6 of Law 2010 mentions that the Authority aims to ensure compliance with laws and regulations related to securities activities. However, Kuwaiti Law 2010 distinguishes between the Authority's right to bring a civil or commercial case and referring the complaint to a public prosecutor. The complaint is for any law, while the former is limited to the Act 2010. It would be better if the authority's powers were extended to all laws that apply to the financial markets and not just securities laws.

---

[130] Qatari Law 2012, Article 32.

[131] ibid Article 39.

4.2 Rule Making by a Regulatory Authority

Rules are part of the legal and regulatory framework.[132] This section will talk about the advantages and disadvantages of rulemaking.

Secondary legislation has advantages:[133]

> 1) Saving parliamentary time, since rules are made without Parliament's involvement. Rules are an alternative to Acts of Parliament. Accordingly, they reduce the statutory burden.[134]

> 2) Speed, by avoiding the lengthy stages involved in parliamentary procedures. Whilst having the force of law, rules are quicker to pass than a statute.

> 3) Expertise needed in complicated areas. For example, making rules that regulate the economy

---

[132] Paul Nelson (n 117) 3-4.

[133] < http://www.lawmentor.co.uk/resources/essays/discuss-advantages-delegated-legislation-form-law-making/> accessed 28 February 2015.

[134] Paul Nelson (n 117) 20.

requires an understanding of how the economy operates.

Alexander Justham, the chief executive of the London Stock Exchange, emphasised the importance of rules by saying that 'one of the crucial roles any regulator plays is to examine the marketplace and potentially intervene through rule changes to ensure that an appropriate equilibrium is consistently achieved'.[135]

In addition to these advantages, a regulatory authority can impose civil fines for violations. For instance, in the UK, the FCA can impose a fine of any amount for breaching the rules. It is a disciplinary function. However, in Kuwait, the authority cannot impose any civil sanctions. Both civil and criminal sanctions should be available for effective enforcement,[136] because the burden of proof required to impose a criminal sanction is higher than the burden to

---

[135] Article entitled 'New Listing Rules Protect Investors and Safeguard London's Open Markets' (2013) <http://www.cityam.com/article/1384224375/new-listing-rules-protect-investors-and-safeguard-london-s-open-markets> accessed 18 January 2014.

[136] Ana Carvajal and Jennifer Elliott (n 120) 19.

impose a civil sanction. Administrative (civil) sanctions differ from criminal fines sanctions. For example, in Kuwait the Capital Market Authority has to refer to the court in order to impose fines. However, there is a limit of 100,000KD for criminal fines. This difference can be clearly seen from the case in February 2014 against the Chairman of Al Ahli Bank who traded based on inside information related to the shares of Al Ahli Bank. The first instance court fined him 1.5 million KD, but the appeal court reduced this to 100,000 KD.[137]

The disadvantage is that delegated rule-making power could have a negative effect in terms of accountability according to the separation of power.[138] Generally, to prevent abuse of power, the executive, legislative and judiciary's powers should be separate.[139] Rule-making

---

[137] <http://www.reuters.com/article/2014/03/03/ahli-bank-kuwait-court-idUSL6N0M01DK20140303> accessed 2 March 2015.

[138] < http://www.lawteacher.net/free-law-essays/english-legal-system/uk-constitution-excessive-concentration-of-power.php> accessed 1 March 2015.

[139] <http://www.essay.uk.com/free-resources/essays/law/constitution-prerogative-powers.php> accessed 1 March 2015.

power results in legislation which has not been fully debated in Parliament.[140] Generally, the process of passing a law involves the legislature enacting the law, the executive carrying out the law, and the judiciary resolving disputes about the law. If the law is not clear, judges must interpret the law and, if there is an ambiguity, determine the meaning of the law.[141] However, courts will not question a law enacted by Parliament if the law is clear and unambiguous.

However, the situation with secondary legislation is different. The courts are not competent to interpret rules, because the courts would need to understand the regulatory authority's views, intentions and policy.[142] However, a court has the power to strike down a secondary regulation if the regulator exceeds its sphere of competence.[143]

---

[140] Emily Finch and Stefan Fafinski (n 118) 11.

[141] <http://cw.routledge.com/textbooks/9780415566957/legislation.asp> accessed 1 March 2015.

[142] Paul Nelson (n 117) 5-6.

[143] <http://www.lawmentor.co.uk/resources/essays/delegated-legislation-controlled-parliament-itself-and-judges-explain-judicial-controls-delegated-legislation/> accessed 1 March 2015.

Conclusion

This book analysed the concept of securities law by looking at the areas of securities, securities law and financial regulation and system.

Undertaking the research for this book was made more complicated for three reasons. First, securities law is among the most complex and misunderstood areas of law. There are a lot of conflicting ideas about securities law. Not surprisingly, some describe securities law as a puzzle.[144] Secondly, in Kuwait, Qatar and Saudi countries, this subject is poorly documented. These factors have made this study more complicated. Another difficulty of this book is that financial laws and regulations in the markets under consideration namely the UK, Kuwait, Qatar and Saudi have been continually changing during the course of this

---

[144] Securities law has a reputation for being one of the most difficult areas of law. In particular, the Securities Act 1933 in the US is so complex that students and lawyers cannot master it on their own; Larry Soderquist and Theresa Gabaldon, *Securities Law* (5th edn, Foundation Press 2014)1.

research, especially because of the global financial crisis of 2008.

In the field of financial regulation, both the UK (common law system)[145] and the Gulf (civil and Shari'ah legal system) have clear rules despite having different legal systems, which has made a comparison easier.

---

[145] For example, in the UK, an act of parliament is higher than case law. In common law system countries such as the UK, parliament can be described as the highest law-making court above any other. Ulrike Muessig, 'Superior Court in Early-Modern France, England and the Holy Roman Empire' in Paul Brand and Joshua Getzler (eds), *Judges and Judging in the History of the Common Law and Civil Law* (CUP 2012) 220.

Bibliography

Ana Carvajal, Jennifer Elliott, The Challenge of Enforcement in Securities Markets: Mission Impossible? (International Monetary Fund (IMF) working paper 2009.

Dalvinder Singh, *Banking Regulation of the UK and the US Financial Markets* (Ashgate 2007).

David L Ratner and Thomas Lee Hazen, *Securities Regulation in a Nutshell* (10th edn, Thomson West 2009).

Emily Finch, Stefan Fafinski, *English Legal System* (4th edn, Pearson 2013).

Emma Murphy and Stephen Senior, 'Changes to the Bank of England' (2013) 20 <http://www.bankofengland.co.uk/publications/Documents/quarterlybulletin/2013/qb130102.pdf> accessed 4 April 2014.

Elham Wahid Daham, *The Effectiveness of the Performance of Capital Markets and Banking Sector in Economic Growth* (National Center For Legal Publications 2013)

Gene Brewer, Richard Walker, 'Red Tape: The Bane of Public Organisations?' in Richard Walker, George Boye and Gene Brewer (eds) *Public Management and Performance: Research Directions* (Cambridge University Press 2010)

Iain G Macneil, *An Introduction to The Law on Financial Investment* (2nd edn, Hart Publishing Ltd 2012)

Ian Bartte and Peter Vass, 'Self-Regulation and the Regulatory State: a Survey of Policy and Practice' (University of Bath, Research Report 17)

Larry Soderquist and Theresa Gabaldon, *Securities Law* (5th edn, Foundation Press 2014)1.

Muhammed Ali Sweilem, *Tools To Invest In the Stock Exchange* (Dar University Publications 2013)

Mohammed Choukri Aladawa, *Stock Exchange in the Balance of Islamic Law* (Dar Thought University 2012)

Mohamed Helmy Abdel Tawab, *The Legality and Technical Frames For The Stock Exchange and Mechanisms of the Legality Observation* (Dar Al Fikr Al Arabi 2012)

Mokhtar Hamida, *Privatisation Through The Financial Markets* (Hassan Modern Library 2013)

Montasser Hamouda, *Economic Crimes* (Dar Elgamaa Elgadida 2010)

Nicholas Ryder, Margaret Griffiths and Lachmi Singh, *Commercial Law: Principles And Policy* (CUP 2012)

Paul Brand and Joshua Getzler (eds), *Judges and Judging in the History of the Common Law and Civil Law* (CUP 2012).

Paul Nelson, *Capital Markets Law and Compliance: the Implications of MiFID* (Cambridge University Press 2011)

Robert Baxt, Ashley Black and Pamela Hanrahan, *Securities and Financial Services Law* (6th LexisNexis 2012)

Robert Shiller, 'Financial Market 2011' (Open Yale University courses I Tunes).

Rodney Hobson, *Shares Made Simple: A Beginner's Guide to the Stock Market* (2nd edn, Hamman House 2012)

Sarah Clarke, *Insider Dealing: Law and Practice* (Oxford University Press 2013)

Steve Bloor, 'After 25 Years of Regulation are consumers better protected?' (2013) <http://www.ifaonline.co.uk/ifaonline/opinion/2258975/after-25-years-of-regulation-are-consumers-better-protected> accessed 14 January 2014.

Stuart Bazley, *Market Abuse Enforcement and Procedure* (Bloomsbury Professional 2013)

Tamer Saleh, *Legal Protection for Securities Markets* (Dar New University 2011)

Thomas Anthony Guerriero, *How to Understand and Master Securities Laws & Regulations* (E- Books 2012, iPad)

Zaid Aboa, *Management of Public Institutions: Foundations of the application of administrative functions* (Dar Al Shorouk 2009)

FCA Article 'Fighting Financial Crime'
<http://www.fca.org.uk/about/what/protecting/financial-crime > accessed 2 January 2014.

Financial Markets and Services Bill, 6.
<http://www.parliament.uk/documents/commons/lib/research/rp99/rp99-068.pdf> accessed 13 January 2014.

<http://www.bankofengland.co.uk/pra/pages/default.aspx> accessed 11 January 2014.

<http://www.bath.ac.uk/management/cri/pubpdf/Research_Reports/17_Bartle_Vass.pdf> accessed 11 February 2014.

<http://cw.routledge.com/textbooks/9780415566957/legislation.asp> accessed 1 March 2015.

<http://www.essay.uk.com/free-resources/essays/law/constitution-prerogative-powers.php> accessed 1 March 2015.

<http://www.fca.org.uk/about/how-we-are-funded/fees> accessed 2 January 2014.

<http://www.fca.org.uk/about/structure> accessed 11 January 2014.

<http://www.imf.org/external/np/sta/wgsd/pdf/051309.pdf> accessed 15 February 2015.

< http://www.investopedia.com/terms/s/security.asp> accessed 16 February 2015.

<http://www.iosco.org/library/pubdocs/pdf/IOSCOPD323. pdf> accessed 26 February 2014.

< http://www.lawmentor.co.uk/resources/essays/discuss-advantages-delegated-legislation-form-law-making/> accessed 28 February 2015.

< http://www.lawteacher.net/free-law-essays/english-legal-system/uk-constitution-excessive-concentration-of-power.php> accessed 1 March 2015.

<http://www.londonstockexchange.com/traders-and-brokers/security-types/security-types.htm> accessed 16 February 2015.

<https://www.moneyadviceservice.org.uk/en/articles/investing-in-shares> accessed 17 January 2015.

<http://www.nyx.com/en/who-we-are/history/new-york> accessed 11 February 2014.

<http://publicappointmentscommissioner.independent.gov. uk/> accessed 22 February 2014.

<http://www.publications.parliament.uk/pa/ld200809/ldsele
ct/ldeconaf/101/10108.htm> accessed 11 January 2014.

<http://www.qfma.org.qa/App_Themes/AR/ABook/Introdu
ction_to_capital_markets.pdf> accessed 16 March 2014.

<http://www.reuters.com/article/2014/03/03/ahli-bank-
kuwait-court-idUSL6N0M01DK20140303> accessed 2
March 2015.

<http://www.soas.ac.uk/library/subjects/law/research/file70
251.pdf > accessed 28 February 2015.

<http://webarchive.nationalarchives.gov.uk/+/http://www.h
m-
treasury.gov.uk/newsroom_and_speeches/press/2001/press
_144_01.cfm> accessed 11 January 2014.

<http://www.youtube.com/watch?v=s5Eoy988728>
accessed 20 May 2014.

www.ingramcontent.com/pod-product-compliance
Lightning Source LLC
Chambersburg PA
CBHW060410190526
45169CB00002B/843